HONEY & HEARTBREAK

Elana Monteleone

First published by Busybird Publishing 2020

Copyright © 2020 Elana Monteleone

ISBN 978-1-922465-03-0

This book is copyright. Apart from any fair dealing for the purposes of study, research, criticism, review, or as otherwise permitted under the Copyright Act, no part may be reproduced by any process without written permission. Enquiries should be made through the publisher.

This is a work of fiction. Any similarities between places and characters are a coincidence.

Cover image: Elana Monteleone

Cover design: Elana Monteleone

Layout and typesetting: Busybird Publishing

Busybird Publishing
2/118 Para Road
Montmorency, Victoria
Australia 3094
www.busybird.com.au

*To the heartbroken,
the hopeful,
and those who have fallen in love alone,
I dedicate this book.*

Honey & Heartbreak

Sweet nectar

the taste on my tongue

of juice escaped

from a golden plum

with amber skin

firm and strong

soft flesh

a surprise delight

drought must end

to bear fruit

rain brings

honey and heartbreak

There comes a time when you are forced to confront everything you have hidden. The truth. The unravelling truth. The burdening truth that you have masked for years. A stunting, stifling, strangling truth scraping at the cage to be freed. When the latch is lifted, relief is instant.

Shy

Well practiced at aversion,
she swiftly avoids her gaze.
With eyes lowered,
a fiery warmth fills her face.
Crimson blush reveals her hand,
timorous but wanting.
She is exposed.

Secret Words

There are words I can never dream to tell you.
And that's life sometimes, I suppose.
I didn't know what it meant when I met you.
I didn't know what good it could hold.
While you couldn't possibly think of me the same way;
In the end it doesn't really matter.
To be a friend, or a lover, or a stranger;
Time with you is cherished all the same.
What I can't say to you I can only feel.
And what I feel I couldn't dare show.
There are words I can never dream to tell you.
And that's life sometimes, I suppose.
I didn't know what it meant when I met you.
But it was worth the bittersweet blow.

To Yearn

A masochistic pursuit
of longing and desire.
An inescapable ache
a burden on every hour.
An unquenchable thirst
never to be indulged.
A truth seldom spoken –
the anguish of my heart.

Hope and cynicism. The dreamer and the realist. The black eyes and the blue tears. The one who flies and the one who flees. Every day, we decide which one to be.

Loveless

I cannot write
of a love returned
it is a joy unknown to me.
I can only relate
to an anxious first date
with someone I'll never again see.

Find Me

Patience is a painful wait
in the still of night
burning eyes, wide-awake
asking when it will find me
what should I change?
where do I go?
I replay the curious plea
how long will it take?
before I wake
with someone there beside me?
what do I do?
who do I meet?
for love to finally find me?

Crush

Oh to steal a kiss from your lips!

And be consumed by the longing in your touch.

Entranced by the scent of your perfume.

And fall willingly victim to the spell of your embrace.

Enamoured with the intensity of your gaze.

Dizzy with the joy of you.

I Dreamt of You

Last night you appeared in my dream
a vision hungered for in daylight,
plainly beautiful –
just You.
And from a distance I was chasing you
wanting desperately for you to notice me,
be with me,
take me in your arms,
breathe my kiss, deeply –
and eventually,
You did.
By choice you came to me.
(Oh how I wish it were real)
and the memory of it –
sorrowful and sweet,
blurs and fades with each minute that passes.
Until I fall asleep again
I hope that you return.

Morning Arrival

Each morning I wait
with quiet excitement
for your arrival
to be greeted by your smile
and casual conversation
because your very presence
brings me such delight.

Morning Grace

Larger than life,
yet moves with a quiet grace
not realising her beauty.
But her smile lights up a room.
And her laugh brings others glee.
And her sweet generosity restores my faith;
That there is kindness in the world,
for as long as she is in it.

Nightfall

Waking eyes ache

for the sight of you in daylight

but are forced to wait for nightfall

where your soft, pale skin

and chestnut eyes

ignite the dark

filling me with warmth and wanting

and twinkling stars

become mere afterthoughts

to the vision of your face.

Your Chaos

I want to know you.
Find out all of your fears
and what makes you smile
where you want to go
and the places you've left behind.

I want your chaos.
All the baggage of your past
and the insecurities you hide
the things you feel ashamed of
whatever they are.

I want your desire.
To see you blush
and writhe in anticipation
to hold your body when it shakes
stealing passion from your lips.

I want your time.
Endless hours and days
each as good as the last
until we can give no more
whenever that may be.

I want you.
All of you.
Every beauty and imperfection.
Every success and every flaw.
For as long as I can have you.

If you don't make it count, be prepared to go without.
You are just a drop in the ocean. In a swiping sea of
disposable profiles, your face is quickly forgotten.

Blister

Beat with caution

dear heart –

do not run

the flame dances

only to lure you

like warmth from the sun,

she smiles

only to burn you.

A Moment

My kiss gives you a part of me
my heart is on my sleeve
anxious eyes laid on you
with hope, you'll never leave

Nothing lasts forever
not even the truest love
because time will pass
and that, my dear –
is something we cannot change.

So I hold on to a moment
however fleeting it may be
because a future with you, my darling
is something I may never see.

Blue

Ocean eyes pierce through me
with an intensity I can't explain
and I'm cracked to wreck and ruin
because I'm vulnerable to pain
but the magnetism of your gaze
holds me in your embrace
ignoring the reality
of the inevitable end we face.

The Heart

The heart is a forgetful fool.
It dismisses the memory of devastation.
Of the weakness that overwhelms the body when it breaks
and the heaviness that weighs on the soul.
With naïve short-sightedness it neglects to recall
all the time it takes for shattered pieces to bind together again.
It is blinded by optimism.
It forgets it all only to be fooled again.
Cruelly,
over and over it breaks.
And over and over it forgives.
In hopes that one day,
it won't need any more healing.

For a long time, it was easy to live in fantasy. Painting imagined romances on the canvas of my heart. Building futures with unsuspecting faces, unwittingly going about their day. But emotional investment with no return eventually takes its toll. Repressed desire is the key ingredient for loneliness, and years of inaction don't ready you for rejection.

The Switch

Click –

I lost my lucent love.

Bereft

I was left

dazed

in a dull, suspended reality

sluggish and slow

where colours lost luminosity

jolted into silence

buzzing

prickling

without any glow.

A Toast

Two crystal glasses
filled with dancing gold liquid
brimming with hopes and expectations
raised in a toast
"To Love!"
a symbol of how it begins
sparkling and full
until time has its way
leaving them stained and empty.

Not Yet

I don't know why,
but I can't delete your number
even though looming silence
has made it clear
I won't hear from you again
and yet for some reason
I can't let go
it's like I'm stuck on what ifs
unfounded maybes
clinging to blind hope
or imagined romance
perhaps it's desperation
so for now
I'm paralysed to remove you
despite hardly getting to know you
I got to know enough
just long enough

to make it foolishly hard
for some inane reason
I'm glued to regrets
totally beyond my control
and still
I can't let go

The Plea of an Ailing Heart

I long for the freedom to be numb
to the pain that permeates from my heart,
giving rise to a flushed face stained with stinging tears.
And snakes coiled in the pit of my stomach.

From the depths of my soul I beg for emancipation
from the lump that gags and chokes my throat,
strangling words with an unyielding hook.
Lips trembling through a helpless whisper.

With desperation I cry for relief
from wasted love and wants and sorrow,
persistent memories of people past.
Tired efforts of pretending to feel joy.

With hope I wait for my release

of imprisoned thoughts and clouded judgement,

to flow from the corners of my mind to the whites of my paper

where written words have me suffer no more.

It's difficult to know whether to lead with your heart or your head. How much of what happens is within our control anyway? Our future is so heavily dictated by our past, that thinking we have a hand in how things play out is more a fantasy than anything else. And while me might accept that our fate is determined, the emotions born from circumstance weigh so heavily on how we perceive things that we continually question the method and meaning to it all. It makes the ride feel so utterly real. It makes the reflection of our own romances so painfully fascinating.

Mixed Feelings

There is undeniable pleasure
in the times when I remember
spending hours of my day with you.

But the memories are tainted
strained and complicated,
by pangs of unfounded regret.

Because it took no time for me to fall
with no impact on you at all,
and for that, I feel like a fool.

But then again, I resolve
when the ache should grow old,
the memories will be light once again.

Girl

Foolish girl.
You continue to go back to her
giving her space in your heart
in spite of the scars she left you with.

Silly girl.
You pass on someone new
clinging hopelessly to the past
even though she'll never have you.

Poor girl.
Your love is wasted on fantasies
keeping everyone at arms length
to guard yourself from pain.

Someday girl.
You will stop thinking of her
allowing your walls to crumble
letting someone else love all the pieces.

The Precipice

Two girls hand in hand
riddled with self doubt
stand at the edge of the precipice
wondering if either could go without
both too scared to jump
so neither of them do
together they just stand there
taking in the view
and while their grip tightens
so too does the fear
as the choice between do or don't
draws rapidly near.

I caught myself one morning, right in the thick of it, dreamily staring out the window. I was standing – smiling – sandwiched in a peak hour train. Blissfully oblivious to everyone around me. I charged up the stairs to the street. I nodded to the man selling magazines. My feet followed the beat of the music blaring in my ears. The songs had new meaning. It was love's luminosity. When it left, it was stripped from me. I questioned everything. Should I be happy it came to pass? Or would I have been glad to have never felt it?

Kiss

It was after our second kiss
when it kept replaying
over and over in my head
that night
and in the days that followed
feeling an involuntary smile
stretch across my face
yes
it was then
that I became certain,
I had to have your lips again.

Midnight Reverie

At night I recall
how your kiss felt on my lips
the warmth of your breath on my back
and the pressure of your hands on my hips
the way I trembled with desire
when later you fell beside me

For K.A.L

Like a bolt of electricity
that sweet caress
when your fingertips trace my forearm
dancing in circles and dizzying strokes
teasing me with the lightest touch
and you smile because you know
that for all my smarts
your hands hold the power
to steal my words
and take my breath away.

Blush

The memory of your smile
and closed eyes
when you laid your lips to my breast
for that brief bite
will forever make me blush

Come

Wrapped around my neck

smiling at the pressure

thighs tighten

before they shake

tasting honey sweet pleasure

Ecstasy

Sink your fingers in my hips
and pull me closer
tease me
with the promise of your kiss
and a tantalizing pause.
Possessed by desire,
move the hair from my eyes
and trace the length of my jaw with your lips
feel me surrender
to your passion and your strength,
consumed with reckless abandon.

Climax

I can feel your urgency
I can sense your pleasure
just a subtle stroke –
frantic scarlet fervour

They say our sense of smell is one of the most powerful memory triggers. That's why I'm glad you didn't wear perfume. If I am to forget the intimate moments, I will do well without the reminder of your scent.

Tripped

There's still a tiny stain
of blood left on my shoe
from the night I tripped and fell
from staring at you
every time I wear them now
I feel a tugging strain
between my happy little memory –
and a heart filled with pain.

Unspoken

I had the urge, you know.
To say it.
Those three little words.
It was one Sunday morning.
The last we had.
I woke and kissed your cheek.
I felt them in my mouth,
but didn't say them.
Grappling and fumbling and thinking.
Maybe it was instinct.
I knew I'd be here,
with the feeling I have now.
Heaviness in my chest,
weightlessness in my arms,
a dull headache,
from crying too long.
But I felt it.

The bliss while it lasted,
the devastation now.
So I guess for me,
you'll always be
the first girl
I couldn't love.

I don't remember what song was playing. Even though the music was loud I heard no sound. But I could see. I can still see. And as I watched the scene unravel before me, I knew the alcohol had not numbed me in the way I hoped it would.

Off Milk

Nourished souls

don't need saving

from soured, spoiled milk

stinging stench, curdled breath

of soured, spoiled milk

rancid, murky memories

beyond the use-by date,

strangling acidity

milk's foul fate

rapture from cloy replies

breeds pathogenic spores

saccharine memories

gone, evermore.

Rebound

That's it, I'm done.
I've have had enough time to think
so come on now, pass me a drink.
Who gives a shit about tomorrow?
Tonight I want to drown my sorrow.
Come over here girl, how about a kiss?
(distract me from the one I actually miss)
Are you here with friends?
Or are you on your own?
Come back to mine,
have your mind blown.
Life's too short for regrets
come on, I'll get you wet
it doesn't matter if I'll be thinking of you
isn't this what all the lonely people do?
A shallow search for adoration,
an ego boost without complication?

Who cares if people think we should
(for a little while we can feel good)
so come on now, girl
come on, let's go
let's lose ourselves in a narcissistic show
of false affections and empty sex
one night with you
I'll forget my ex.

Poison

Confess
broken hearted lover
when chemicals kicked in
only green glowed
in your eyes
through your bloodstream

It's not just sadness. It's faithless, numb indifference. It swims beneath the surface, waiting. Anaesthesia coursing through my veins. It knows my triggers. It waits for the tear and leaks out. Black, throbbing indecision. Dark, disorienting drips. Humour hides in horror. Wonder can't be woken. It pulls me in a chokehold. Temporarily persistent. And all I can do is reach.

Smile

Sometimes it's real.

For a minute or two,

it happens unconsciously.

Spreading with ease across my face.

Where stiff muscles

relax and melt –

lighting my eyes,

blushing my cheeks –

and relief washes over,

unadulterated bliss!

Weightlessness washes over my entire body.

But just as quickly, it fades.

And dark clouds loom again.

Closing in over me,

cold and heavy.

But through the melancholy I try to keep the smile there.

Even if it's artificial and strained –

because levity always comes.
And even as I wait;
somewhere,
hidden in the pain,
I remind myself
there is still beauty.

Playtime

I have this little habit
of talking circles in my head
running over past conversations
and things I should have said
in a spiral of rumination
I keep going back and forth
but it always ends the same
for whatever time its worth
and despite the same conclusions
I continue to this day
with the agony of contemplation
in my masochistic game

Meaningless

Ever it will, ever it could

everything happens as it should

until the day you're laid to rest

you'll delude yourself it was all a test

but as old philosophers once told

happiness is a lie we're sold

because when your heart finally stops beating

so clearly you'll see, every joy was fleeting.

The Act

Come one, come all!
To the illusory parade
see her dance
see her laugh
enjoy the charade.

Watch the lines
watch them grow
of people here
to see the show.

She twists
she turns
she wins their favour
an ornamental act
for fools to savour.

Her words are empty

her smile is fake,

but they haven't a care,

they take,

they take!

Our Fate

We are the walking dead
the end is preordained
choice is an illusion
not so, is your pain
when our lives have no meaning
what keeps breath sustained?
do explain to me,
the simple recipe;
Blind hope for happiness
a tired pursuit of love
and steadfast denial
of the truth of one's trial.

How readily we accept rejection, but question love. Without hesitance we believe hateful slurs and words fuelled by anger. Yet we doubt the motives of those who offer praise or kindness. We cling to memories of devastation, replaying them in the quiet hours of the night. Why do we not focus on the amusement of the everyday? Of swift smiles exchanged between strangers or the feel of the sun on our skin in springtime? We are addicted to pain. Happiness may only be temporary, but our memories of it linger for as long as we allow them. We choose our focus. Just as we choose our worth.

Park Bench in Winter

Sitting on a park bench.
The air is cold.
A stranger sits near with a book.

Despite frosted fingers
I do not move.
Enjoying the artificial company.

The sun beams down
an unexpected warmth
and a small smile escapes.

I think I'll stay
just a little while longer
and see what else should come of it.

New Year

And just like that
the countdown ends
and coloured embers light the sky
couples kiss in sweet embrace
with new hopes freed to fly.

Acknowledgements

It would be far-fetched of me to suggest that all of the poems in this book are fictional, so it goes without saying that writing this little poetry book and getting it published has certainly been a labour of love and indeed, heartbreak! It took around three years to write and an additional six months to decide whether or not to do anything with it. Eventually, the continual prods of encouragement from close friends and family prompted me to bite the bullet and send my manuscript to the wonderful team at BusyBird Publishing to be printed.

With that said, the first acknowledgement I need to give is somewhat of an awkward one, because it is to someone I no longer see but feel compelled to recognise. K.A.L, not all of the poems in this book are about you, but it would be remiss of me to ignore the impact you had on so many of the pieces. You opened my eyes to the complex emotions that surround a first love; I have nothing but gratitude for the time we spent together and the scintillatingly knotty inspiration you gifted me with.

To Archimede Fusillo, please accept my heartfelt thanks for taking the time to read my draft manuscript and offer feedback. It meant the world to me to have an established author express faith in my story. Without your words of encouragement, I would have continued to allow this story to gather dust on my desk.

Lastly, I would like to thank my loving family; my parents, Terese and Rudy; sister Rachael and my brother-in-law Robert. There is no denying that many of the poems in this book were born from very challenging and dark emotions. In those times especially, you offered me the support and love only a family can. Without each of you, I would not have found the strength to transform my emotions into something that could work for me, instead of against me. To Mum especially (because you love poetry the most!) thank you for being my number one fan.

About the author

Elana Monteleone was born in Melbourne, Australia in 1991. She attended RMIT University and graduated in 2012 with a Bachelor of Communication (Advertising).

Since graduating, she has worked as a web writer and content producer and began writing poetry as a creative release in 2016. Honey & Heartbreak is her first published poetry book.

www.ingramcontent.com/pod-product-compliance
Lightning Source LLC
Chambersburg PA
CBHW071756080526
44588CB00013B/2259